Contents

Age of dinosaurs

Dinosaurs appeared about 245 million years ago (mya). Along with their relatives, they were the dominant animals on Earth until 65 million years ago.

During this time, the climate was generally warmer than it is today, and the continents were all joined together. Other types of animals were also around, but dinosaurs were the largest, fastest, and most fearsome creatures on the land.

Pangaea
When dinosaurs first appeared, Earth was made up of a single continent called Pangaea. About 175 million years ago, the continental plates began to split up and they slowly drifted apart.

Meet Triceratops

Triceratops lived 68–65 million years ago in what is now North America. It was a plant-eating dinosaur that looked like a modern rhinoceros. It had the misfortune to share its living space with one of the most terrifying dinosaurs ever to have lived—Tyrannosaurus rex—which liked to eat Triceratops.

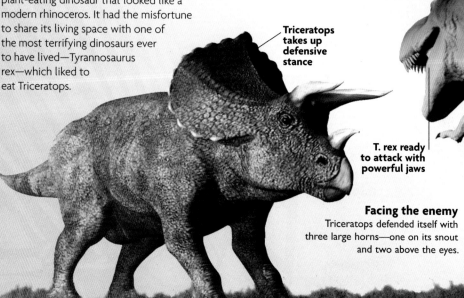

Triceratops takes up defensive stance

T. rex ready to attack with powerful jaws

Facing the enemy
Triceratops defended itself with three large horns—one on its snout and two above the eyes.

Timeline

	Triassic period	Jurassic period	Cretaceous period		
	Dinosaurs and mammals evolve	Birds evolve		Dinosaurs become extinct	Humans appear

MESOZOIC ERA			CENOZOIC ERA	
248 mya	206 mya	144 mya	65 mya	2.5 mya

The big three
These three dinosaurs were the giants of their time. Brachiosaurus was 85 feet long and 50 feet tall; Iguanodon grew up to 33 feet and reached a height of 9 feet; T. rex was about 40 feet long and 20 feet tall.

Long neck to reach treetops

Dinosaur groups
There are two main groups of dinosaurs: saurischians (lizard-hipped) and ornithischians (bird-hipped). Saurischians include plant-eaters like Diplodocus and meat-eaters like T. rex; ornithischians include armored, boneheaded, duck-billed, and horned dinosaurs like Triceratops.

Powerful muscular body

Spiky, conical thumbs

**Brachiosaurus
154 mya**

**Iguanodon
125 mya**

**T. rex
68 mya**

Head balanced behind by a large tail

The first dinosaur
The earliest known dinosaur-like creature was Nyasasaurus, which lived about 243 million years ago. It measured 10 feet from head to tail and stood on two legs. Parts of its skeleton were found near Lake Nyasa (Malawi) in Tanzania—the place after which it is named.

Other Mesozoic creatures

During the Mesozoic era, many other types of animals shared the world with dinosaurs.

There were small mammals that hid from the meat-eating dinosaurs, and larger mammals that fed on dinosaur eggs. Giant fish swam the oceans and huge frogs lived on the shores. Many giant reptiles roamed the seas or flew in the air.

Pterosaurs

These were the first animals with a backbone that could fly rather than glide. The smallest pterosaurs were the size of a sparrow. The largest was Quetzalcoatlus, which had a 36-foot wingspan—the same as that of a light aircraft. But it hunted on the ground, crawling up to prey and stabbing at it like a modern stork.

The head crest was unique to pterosaurs.

Plesiosaurs

These marine reptiles were slow swimmers, but were able to catch fish. The small heads on their long necks could sneak up on a shoal of fish before the pressure wave from their bodies could warn the fish away.

Many ichthyosaurs had dorsal fins.

Ichthyosaurs

These marine reptiles looked like modern dolphins. They had large eyes that probably helped them to dive deep into the murky waters and catch fast-swimming prey. Some grew up to 50 feet long.

Prehistoric mammals and fish

Repenomamus
Not all mammals hid from dinosaurs. In fact, some were out hunting dinosaurs. Repenomamus was 3 feet long, and fed on dinosaur babies.

Beelzebufo
The world's largest ever frog was about 16 inches across—the size of a beach ball—and resembled a horned toad. Its giant mouth could have gobbled up young dinosaurs.

Leedsichthys
In the ocean, this 50-foot-long fish ate tiny creatures by sucking in water and filtering them through its gills. It was the world's largest ever fish with a bony skeleton.

Mosasaurs

Mosasaurs were large marine reptiles with short necks and enormous jaws lined with sharp teeth. Their bite was four times more powerful than that of a T. rex. They were built to chase fast-swimming fish and sharks. After the ichthyosaurs died out, mosasaurs became the top predators in Mesozoic seas.

Flippers were used for swimming.

5

Clues to a lost world

We know what dinosaurs looked like from their fossils, which are the preserved impressions of their bodies found in rocks.

Most fossil finds are of isolated parts, such as a tooth or bone, although sometimes the preserved fossils of entire skeletons and even soft tissue have been found. Nevertheless, even the smallest fragment can be enough to tell an experienced paleontologist (a scientist who studies fossils) the type of dinosaur it came from, what it looked like, and even how it lived its life.

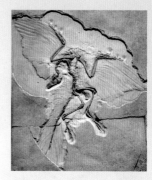

▲ This fossil of Archaeopteryx was found in Germany. Many consider Archaeopteryx to be the first bird on Earth.

1. Death
A stegosaur dies on the bank of a river.

2. Buried
The remains are covered by mud before it can be eaten or disturbed.

How do fossils form?

When an animal dies, the body is covered with sediment before it has time to decay and break down. Sediment can be mud in a river, sand in a desert, or ash from a volcanic eruption. Over time, the body falls apart and dissolves. The mud, sand, or ash then hardens into rock, preserving an impression of the body.

Pieces of a puzzle

Paleontologists have to work slowly and carefully to free a fossilized skeleton from rock, and use power drills, pick axes, trowels, and brushes. Back in the laboratory or museum, they piece the animal together. Triceratops, for example, has 312 bones—106 more than human beings—so it's similar to solving a giant 3-D puzzle. It can take months to build the skeleton, but once finished, it shows the size and shape of the dinosaur.

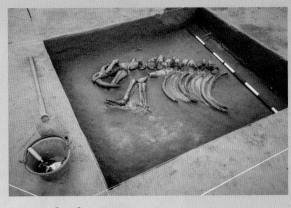

Digging for dinosaurs
Scientists try to keep the fossil bones together while they dig.

▶ This fossilized claw is from the hind foot of a meat-eating dinosaur. It is about 7 inches long.

3. Compressed
The layers of mud are compressed and form rock; chemical processes take place that preserve the skeleton.

4. Fossilized
The stegosaur's bones turn to stone, and remain in the rock for millions of years. This process can also preserve tracks in mud and dinosaur droppings.

Where in the world?

Dinosaur fossils have been unearthed on every continent, which isn't surprising, as Pangaea was a single landmass. Here are the sites in which some of the key fossils were found.

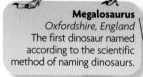

Megalosaurus
Oxfordshire, England
The first dinosaur named according to the scientific method of naming dinosaurs.

T. rex "Sue"
South Dakota
The most complete T. rex fossil ever to be found.

North America

Triceratops
Colorado
The most dominant plant-eater of its time.

Giganotosaurus
Patagonia, Argentina
One of the largest meat-eaters that ever lived.

South America

Archaeopteryx
Solnhofen, Germany
The ancestor of modern birds.

Dreadnoughtus
Patagonia, Argentina
The largest land animal that ever lived.

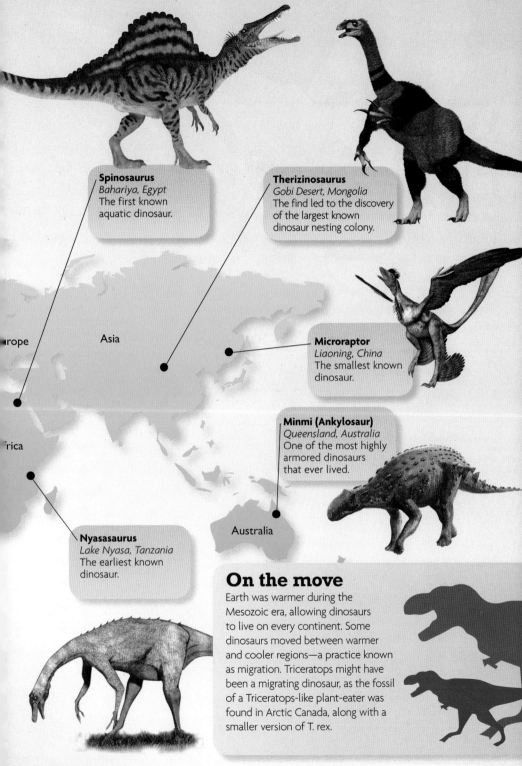

Spinosaurus
Bahariya, Egypt
The first known aquatic dinosaur.

Therizinosaurus
Gobi Desert, Mongolia
The find led to the discovery of the largest known dinosaur nesting colony.

Microraptor
Liaoning, China
The smallest known dinosaur.

Minmi (Ankylosaur)
Queensland, Australia
One of the most highly armored dinosaurs that ever lived.

Nyasasaurus
Lake Nyasa, Tanzania
The earliest known dinosaur.

rope

Asia

rica

Australia

On the move

Earth was warmer during the Mesozoic era, allowing dinosaurs to live on every continent. Some dinosaurs moved between warmer and cooler regions—a practice known as migration. Triceratops might have been a migrating dinosaur, as the fossil of a Triceratops-like plant-eater was found in Arctic Canada, along with a smaller version of T. rex.

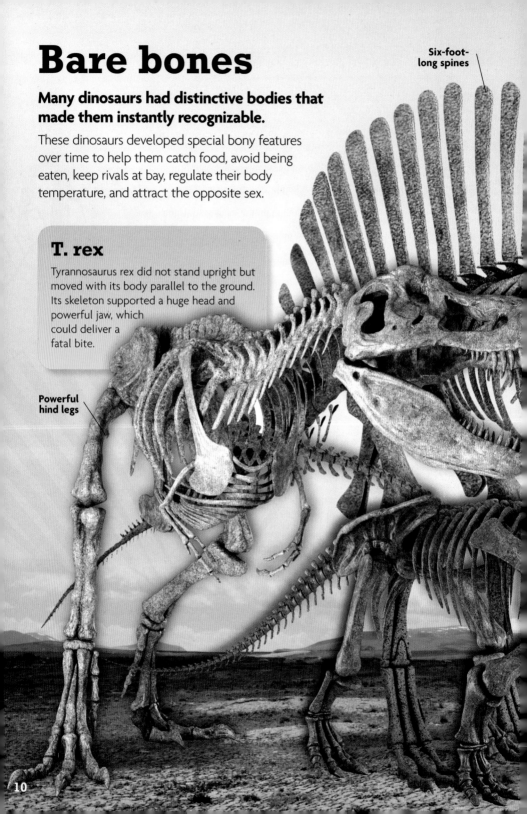

Bare bones

Many dinosaurs had distinctive bodies that made them instantly recognizable.

These dinosaurs developed special bony features over time to help them catch food, avoid being eaten, keep rivals at bay, regulate their body temperature, and attract the opposite sex.

Six-foot-long spines

T. rex

Tyrannosaurus rex did not stand upright but moved with its body parallel to the ground. Its skeleton supported a huge head and powerful jaw, which could deliver a fatal bite.

Powerful hind legs

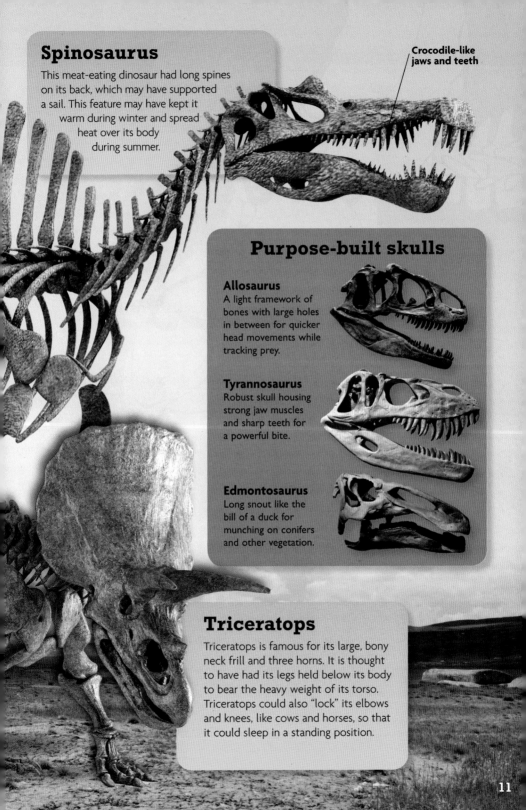

Spinosaurus

This meat-eating dinosaur had long spines on its back, which may have supported a sail. This feature may have kept it warm during winter and spread heat over its body during summer.

Crocodile-like jaws and teeth

Purpose-built skulls

Allosaurus
A light framework of bones with large holes in between for quicker head movements while tracking prey.

Tyrannosaurus
Robust skull housing strong jaw muscles and sharp teeth for a powerful bite.

Edmontosaurus
Long snout like the bill of a duck for munching on conifers and other vegetation.

Triceratops

Triceratops is famous for its large, bony neck frill and three horns. It is thought to have had its legs held below its body to bear the heavy weight of its torso. Triceratops could also "lock" its elbows and knees, like cows and horses, so that it could sleep in a standing position.

Muscle power

The larger dinosaurs had thick muscles attached to their bones, which made them strong and powerful.

Although the existence of fossilized dinosaur muscles is rare, experts can figure out how they were arranged by looking at the marks on fossil bones, where muscles had been anchored. They've also compared them to the muscles of modern birds and reptiles—the living relatives of dinosaurs.

Biting muscles

Triceratops used three types of muscles to open and close its jaws. It opened its mouth by shortening the muscles of the lower jaw, while another snapped the jaws shut. The muscles around the mouth gave Triceratops a powerful bite.

Jaw muscle

Muscles around the mouth

Muscles for moving

Triceratops had strong leg muscles to carry its heavy body weight. After studying its skeleton and fossilized footprints, scientists know that the legs were underneath the animal, not splayed out like those of lizards. They believe that it would have moved much like a modern black rhinoceros. At maximum speed, Triceratops could have moved along at 35 miles per hour (mph)— about 5 mph faster than a rhino.

Hands and feet

Scientists have studied the fossilized bones of the forelimbs and hind limbs, as well as the nails and claws, to learn how dinosaurs used their limbs.

Plant-eaters
Large plant-eating dinosaurs with horned, plated, or armored bodies had broad, stubby feet to carry their heavy body weight.

Meat-eaters
Some predators had sharp, curved claws on their hands or hind feet, which they used for seizing or slashing prey.

Ornithopods
These dinosaurs had three-toed feet on their hind limbs, with toes ending in blunt nails for extra grip when they ran.

Euoplocephalus

Swinging a forelimb

Five shoulder muscles helped Triceratops move each forelimb back and forth. Shortening two of these muscles (1 and 2) pulled the upper arm forward. Shortening another two (3 and 4) lifted the arm. A fifth muscle (5) hauled it back. The triceps muscle then pulled on the main forearm bone to straighten the arm.

Comparing speeds

In computer simulations, one of the fastest dinosaurs also happens to be one of the smallest. The turkey-sized Compsognathus whizzed along at 40 mph, Velociraptor reached about 30 mph, and T. rex had a top speed of only 18 mph. Usain Bolt—the world's fastest man—could have outrun it with a top speed of 28 mph. The giant sauropods were even slower, moving at 5 mph.

T. rex
18 mph

Compsognathus
40 mph

Triceratops
35 mph

Fastest human
28 mph

▶ Despite their size, many dinosaurs ran faster than us.

| 0 mph | 5 mph | 10 mph | 15 mph | 20 mph | 25 mph | 30 mph | 35 mph | 40 mph |

Nervous system

Dinosaurs controlled their bodies with a nervous system that was much like ours.

The brain and the spinal cord were the main parts of their nervous system. The spinal cord of some of the long-necked plant-eaters was very long indeed. But the cerebrum—the thinking part of the brain—was small in most dinosaurs. The cleverest dinosaur was probably as smart as a bird, but some birds can be pretty clever!

Long nerves

Giant sauropods had the longest nerve cells (cells that carry messages through the nervous system) ever known. A sensory nerve cell would run up to 150 feet from the tail to the brain stem. A signal would have taken half a second to go from one end of the animal to the other.

Second brain?
Early on, scientists falsely believed that giant dinosaurs had a "second brain" in their hips.

Brain size

Although brains do not fossilize well, scientists can figure out the size of dinosaur brains by measuring the size of the area that housed them. The titanosaurs, for example, were the largest land animals that ever lived, but they had brains the size of tennis balls. Meat-eating theropods, such as T. rex, had the biggest brains. Measuring brain size is one way to gauge a dinosaur's intelligence.

Parts of the brain

Some parts of a dinosaur's brain were well developed. This includes the olfactory region which deals with smell, and the cerebellum which helps to coordinate movement. However, the cerebrum, which is large in human beings, was generally small, especially in plant-eaters such as Triceratops.

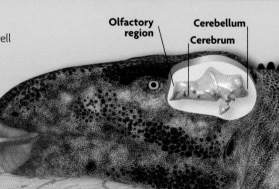

Olfactory region

Cerebellum

Cerebrum

Position of eyes

The eyes of meat-eating dinosaurs were on the front of their face, so the visual field of each eye overlapped. This arrangement allowed them to judge distances of potential prey. The plant-eaters had eyes on the sides of their heads, like modern cattle, giving them a clear sight of their surroundings, so they could spot any approaching predators.

T. rex

Triceratops

Sense of smell and hearing

Like modern predators, the meat-eating dinosaurs had acute senses of smell and hearing. Giant sauropod plant-eaters, on the other hand, did not hear well. But, like modern elephants, they were able to detect low-frequency rumbles and vibrations through the ground.

Big brain
T. rex had a brain the size of a coconut.

Intelligence

Scientists also look at brain size in relation to the body size to measure an animal's potential intelligence. Using this method, scientists have deduced that swift, two-legged meat-eaters such as Velociraptor were among the smartest dinosaurs around.

Heart and lungs

A dinosaur's heart pumped blood through its blood vessels to billions of cells throughout its body.

The blood carried oxygen (from the air that was breathed in) and nutrients (from digested food) to every living cell. These then built new body cells and provided energy to work the muscles. So far, scientists have not been able to understand in any great detail how a dinosaur's heart and lung systems worked, as soft organ tissues rarely fossilize.

▶ As some dinosaurs shared a common ancestor with birds, it's likely that their hearts were similar, indicating that these dinosaurs could have been warm-blooded.

Warm-blooded heart

Pumping hearts

Similar to birds and crocodiles, some dinosaurs probably had a four-chambered heart. The two chambers on one side pumped blood out to the body through arteries, and the other side pulled it back through the veins. However, scientists still cannot explain how a titanosaur's blood system overcame gravity to pump blood to its head many feet above its heart without damaging the organ from the need to produce a very high blood pressure.

Alligator chest cavity

Apatosaurus chest cavity

Measuring chest cavity

Warm-blooded creatures have larger lungs and hearts than cold-blooded animals. In dinosaurs, lung size can be calculated by measuring the size of the chest cavity. The sauropod Apatosaurus, for example, had a deeper cavity than a modern alligator, which suggests that it may have been warm-blooded.

Short and stout body

▶ Triceratops was short and stout, so a relatively low blood pressure would have ensured that blood reached all parts of its body.

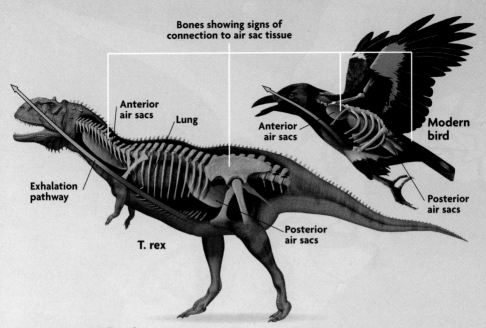

Bones showing signs of
connection to air sac tissue

Anterior
air sacs

Lung

Exhalation
pathway

Posterior
air sacs

T. rex

Anterior
air sacs

Modern
bird

Posterior
air sacs

Lungs and air sacs

The breathing system of some dinosaurs, particularly the fast-moving meat-eaters and the long-necked sauropods, was probably similar to that found in birds. The lungs were linked to a system of air sacs. These sacs allowed dinosaurs to take in oxygen from the air when breathing in and out.

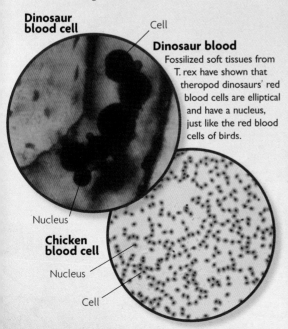

**Dinosaur
blood cell**

Cell

Dinosaur blood

Fossilized soft tissues from T. rex have shown that theropod dinosaurs' red blood cells are elliptical and have a nucleus, just like the red blood cells of birds.

Nucleus

**Chicken
blood cell**

Nucleus

Cell

Warm-blooded or cold-blooded?

The debate over whether dinosaurs were warm- or cold-blooded has yet to be settled. It is possible that some dinosaurs were cold-blooded and others warm-blooded. While the biological link to birds suggests that some dinosaurs were warm-blooded, other dinosaurs had structures on their bodies that were probably used for absorbing or spreading heat, indicating that they were cold-blooded. For example, Spinosaurus had large sails on its back, and Stegosaurus had plates.

Diet of dinosaurs

Some dinosaurs were carnivores (meat-eaters) but a greater number were herbivores (plant-eaters).

The meat-eaters were hunters and scavengers. They fed on creatures as small as insects, raided nests, and even caught fish. The plant-eaters were either browsers, feeding on trees and bushes, or grazers that munched on low-growing shrubs. Once flowering plants appeared on Earth, the plant-eaters also fed on grasses and fruits.

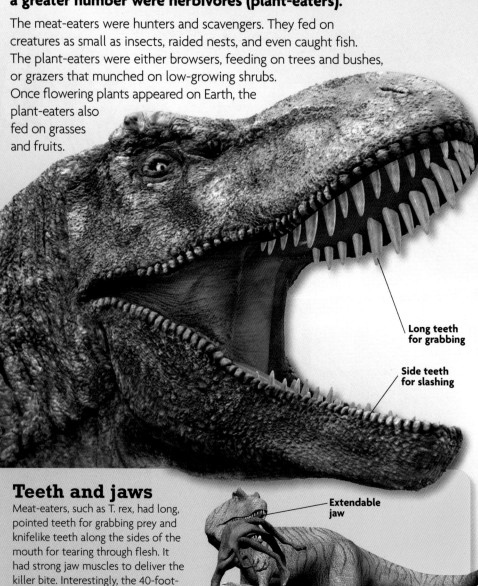

Long teeth for grabbing

Side teeth for slashing

Teeth and jaws

Meat-eaters, such as T. rex, had long, pointed teeth for grabbing prey and knifelike teeth along the sides of the mouth for tearing through flesh. It had strong jaw muscles to deliver the killer bite. Interestingly, the 40-foot-long Allosaurus could extend its tooth-filled jaws outward, like a snake, so it could take an even bigger bite.

Extendable jaw

▲ Allosaurus had dozens of sawlike teeth in its jaws.

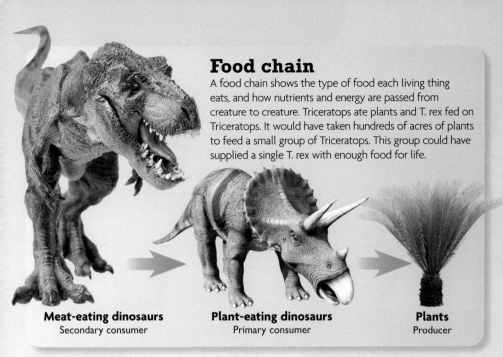

Food chain

A food chain shows the type of food each living thing eats, and how nutrients and energy are passed from creature to creature. Triceratops ate plants and T. rex fed on Triceratops. It would have taken hundreds of acres of plants to feed a small group of Triceratops. This group could have supplied a single T. rex with enough food for life.

Meat-eating dinosaurs
Secondary consumer

Plant-eating dinosaurs
Primary consumer

Plants
Producer

Ways of eating

The theropods had a varied diet. Fossils of Compsognathus and Oviraptor have been found with a lizard in their stomachs. Paleontologists also unearthed a Velociraptor that was buried in the act of attacking a Protoceratops. Scientists know that Spinosaurus, Masiakasaurus, and Baryonyx caught fish. Some theropods fed on plants too. For example, the peacock-like Caudipteryx was an omnivore (animals that eat both plants and meat), and a few, such as Therizinosaurus, a theropod dinosaur with the largest claws of any known animal, were plant-eaters.

▼ This fossil skeleton of Coelophysis shows the bones of a small crocodile-like reptile in its stomach.

Digestive system

Few fossils show the insides of a dinosaur. But from what is known, it is thought that the digestive system of a plant-eater was larger than that of a meat-eater.

Plant-eaters such as Triceratops, along with long-necked sauropods and duck-billed dinosaurs, had large digestive systems to break down the fiber in the plants they ate. Food passed through their long intestine, where bacteria aided digestion by breaking down the tough, fibrous parts of plants.

Stomach has a single chamber.

Gastric stones

At one time it was thought that sauropods swallowed stones, which collected in their stomachs, to help break up plant food. Now scientists believe these polished stones were swallowed accidentally while feeding and played no part in digestion. Some omnivorous theropods, however, did have "gastric stones" like modern birds.

Tough on the teeth

Unlike other plant-eaters, Diplodocus stripped rather than nibbled the leaves from branches, and it ate different plants than Camarasaurus—another sauropod living at the same time. The food, though, was damaging to its teeth, which Diplodocus replaced every 35 days. Most remarkably, Nigersaurus, a close relative of Diplodocus, had teeth that lasted only 14 days before they had to be replaced.

Intestine contains bacteria to break down tough plants.

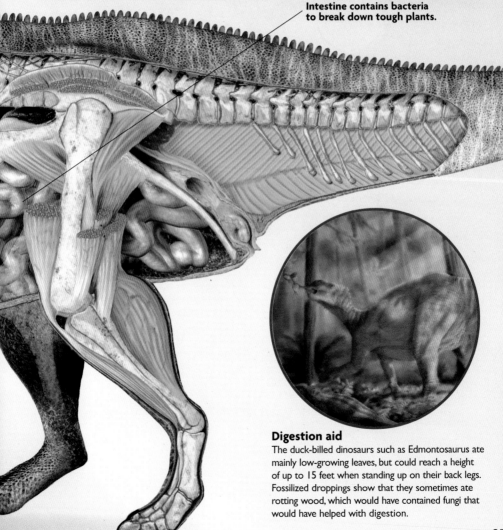

Digestion aid

The duck-billed dinosaurs such as Edmontosaurus ate mainly low-growing leaves, but could reach a height of up to 15 feet when standing up on their back legs. Fossilized droppings show that they sometimes ate rotting wood, which would have contained fungi that would have helped with digestion.

Getting rid of waste

After eating and digesting their food, dinosaurs had to get rid of all the waste products from their bodies.

The kidneys cleaned the blood, forming urine, which passed through their urinary tract and out of the body. Solid waste collected in the intestines and was then expelled in the form of droppings. Fossil droppings are called "coprolites."

Fossilized waste

Scientists study coprolites to find out what a dinosaur ate. For example, coprolites from a tyrannosaur were found to contain the partially digested bones of a young duck-billed dinosaur. It shows that T. rex probably fed on younger animals, which were easier to catch and couldn't fight back. The bone pieces also suggest that T. rex's digestive system was quite short and not as efficient as that of a modern crocodile, which can digest almost everything it swallows.

Dung beetles
Coprolites of a duck-billed dinosaur have been found with tiny tunnels in them. These were made by dung beetles alive at the time of the dinosaurs.

▼ Sauropod dinosaurs produced the largest coprolites. One such fossil measured 14 inches across—thought to be several droppings fused together. The finding indicates that sauropod droppings were probably quite watery.

Natural fertilizer

The giant sauropod dinosaurs ate huge amounts of plant food. The 60-foot-long Mamenchisaurus, for example, ate about 1,150 pounds of vegetation each day—the same weight as about seven adult human beings. These dinosaurs must have deposited enormous quantities of dung. The dung expelled each day worked like manure, and fertilized the forests and grasslands, helping to keep them lush and green.

Desert dinosaurs

Some dinosaurs, such as the fierce, meat-eating Velociraptor, lived in sandy deserts and other arid places, so they must have had to conserve water. Their digestive systems would have been very efficient, extracting every drop of moisture from food and retaining it, so they probably didn't urinate.

Velociraptor

Skin and feathers

There is some debate among paleontologists over what dinosaur skin looked like.

It was thought that many dinosaurs had scaly skin, but recent fossil finds now reveal that many meat-eating dinosaurs had downy, ribbon-shaped, and even brightly colored feathers. Plumes might well have evolved from scales.

▼ Archaeopteryx was the first birdlike dinosaur found with feathers. At first, scientists thought it was an actual bird.

Feathered dinosaurs

Newly discovered fossils of theropod dinosaurs have revealed actual feathers and pits in the skin from which feathers grew. The finding has changed the view of what they looked like and how they behaved. The main function of feathers was to keep the animal warm, or to make it attractive to the opposite sex, but some feathered dinosaurs were able to glide, and maybe even fly.

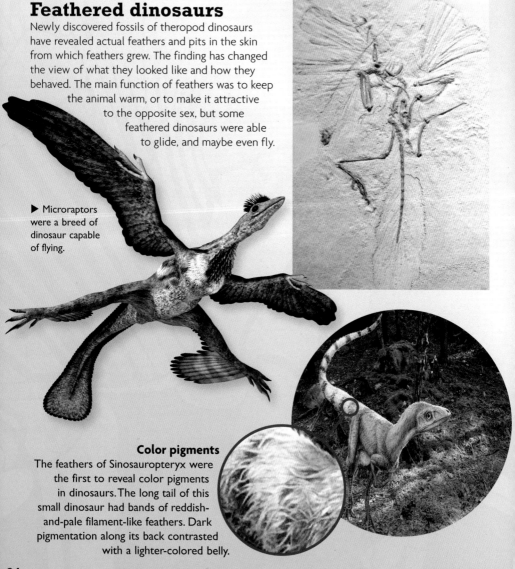

▶ Microraptors were a breed of dinosaur capable of flying.

Color pigments

The feathers of Sinosauropteryx were the first to reveal color pigments in dinosaurs. The long tail of this small dinosaur had bands of reddish-and-pale filament-like feathers. Dark pigmentation along its back contrasted with a lighter-colored belly.

Leaving an impression

Duck-billed dinosaurs that were buried rapidly (perhaps under a mudslide) have well-preserved fossilized skin. They show that these dinosaurs' five-sided scales did not overlap like those of snakes, but lay one next to the other. They also had round or flat bony projections for extra protection. The fossils also show how some duck-billed dinosaurs had soft and fleshy (rather than bony) crests, like a rooster's comb.

◀ It is thought that male dinosaurs were more colorful than females. Many used their color to attract a mate, much like modern animals.

Skin for display

While color pigments have been found in dinosaur feathers, they have yet to be found in their skin. But, like colorful lizards, snakes, and some birds, dinosaurs may well have had brightly colored skin, and those colors could have been even brighter at mating time.

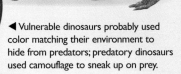

◀ Vulnerable dinosaurs probably used color matching their environment to hide from predators; predatory dinosaurs used camouflage to sneak up on prey.

Skin for disguise

Rather than stick out from the crowd, some dinosaurs may have had skin colors that enabled them to blend in with their background. The giant titanosaurs probably didn't need camouflage because their huge size kept predators away. They were probably a gray color, like elephants and rhinos.

Armor for defense

The first dinosaurs had simple armor, such as bony outer plates called scutes, which we see on modern crocodiles.

Dinosaurs that appeared later on evolved large plates, spikes, clubs, and a covering of heavy armor over their bodies called a carapace. These proved to be a successful defense system for the plant-eaters.

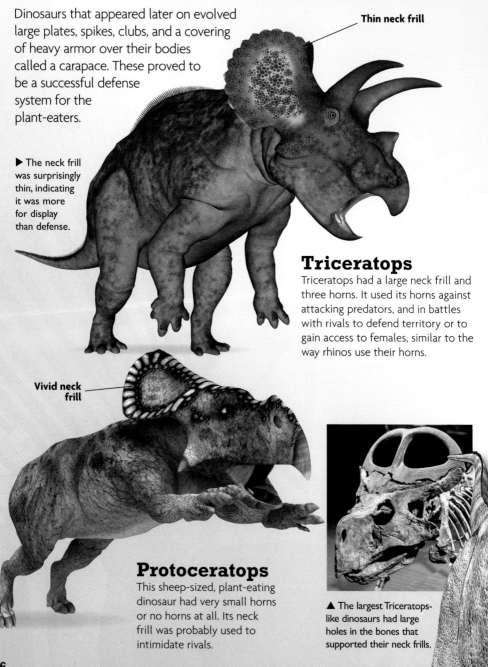

Thin neck frill

▶ The neck frill was surprisingly thin, indicating it was more for display than defense.

Triceratops

Triceratops had a large neck frill and three horns. It used its horns against attacking predators, and in battles with rivals to defend territory or to gain access to females, similar to the way rhinos use their horns.

Vivid neck frill

Protoceratops

This sheep-sized, plant-eating dinosaur had very small horns or no horns at all. Its neck frill was probably used to intimidate rivals.

▲ The largest Triceratops-like dinosaurs had large holes in the bones that supported their neck frills.

Pachycephalosaurus

Extremely thick skull roof

Pachycephalosaurus had a built-in crash helmet. At first it was thought that the males butted heads like mountain sheep rams, but it is more likely that they settled squabbles among themselves by swinging their hard heads against the flanks of their opponent, like male giraffes.

▶ Pachycephalosaurus means "thick-headed lizard."

Display horn for attracting a mate

▶ Ceratosaurus grew to a length of more than 20 feet.

Ceratosaurus

This meat-eating theropod had a blade-like horn on its snout, two small horns on its head, and a prominent ridge in front of each eye. They were probably used as a display to attract a mate at breeding time, so the nasal horn might even have been brightly colored.

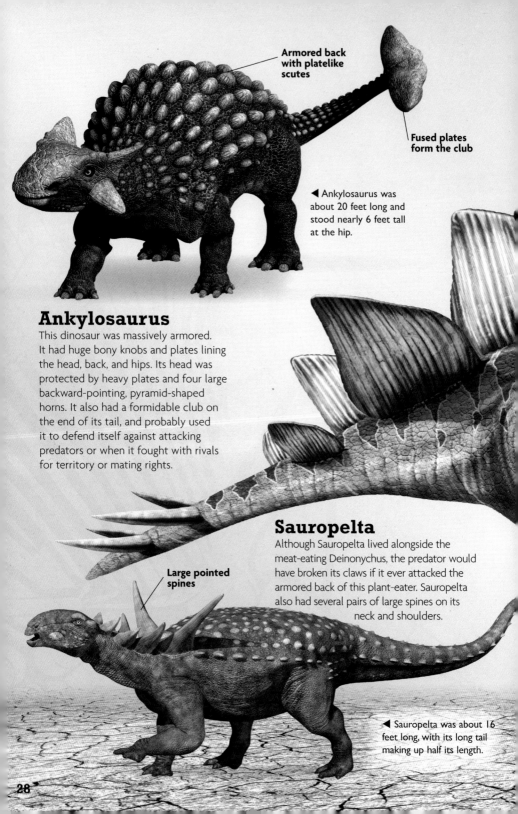

Armored back
with platelike
scutes

Fused plates
form the club

◀ Ankylosaurus was
about 20 feet long and
stood nearly 6 feet tall
at the hip.

Ankylosaurus

This dinosaur was massively armored.
It had huge bony knobs and plates lining
the head, back, and hips. Its head was
protected by heavy plates and four large
backward-pointing, pyramid-shaped
horns. It also had a formidable club on
the end of its tail, and probably used
it to defend itself against attacking
predators or when it fought with rivals
for territory or mating rights.

Sauropelta

Although Sauropelta lived alongside the
meat-eating Deinonychus, the predator would
have broken its claws if it ever attacked the
armored back of this plant-eater. Sauropelta
also had several pairs of large spines on its
neck and shoulders.

Large pointed
spines

◀ Sauropelta was about 16
feet long, with its long tail
making up half its length.

Dangerous tails

Clubs were swung at attackers and were capable of smashing bones and crippling enemies. Spines delivered slashing attacks, inflicting severe injuries. To support such large weapons, the vertebrae (small bones forming the backbone) at the tail end were often fused and supported by large tendons.

Euoplocephalus
This low, wide, armored ankylosaur had a tail like a steel wrecking ball.

Huayangosaurus
With a tail bearing long spines, this stegosaur would have left a three-foot-long wound in its enemies.

Stegosaurus

Stegosaurus had rows of large flat, vertical plates on its back, but they are not thought to have been for defense. The dinosaur repelled its attackers with huge spikes on its tail. The plates could have been used for display, or they could have helped it to control its body temperature, absorbing heat from the morning sun and dispersing it later in the day.

Flat, thin plates on the back

Social or solitary?

Some of the meat-eating dinosaurs probably hunted alone, but there is evidence to suggest that others formed into hunting packs.

Fossil finds have helped paleontologists conclude that some dinosaurs lived in herds while others were lone creatures. Large numbers of skeletons found at a single site indicate that those dinosaurs probably lived together. In contrast, findings of individual footprints suggest that the dinosaurs they belong to roamed alone. Lots of fossil footprints heading in the same direction indicate a herd that was on the move.

Journey marked by footprints

Fossil footprints and trackways reveal dinosaur movements. Large numbers of different-sized fossil footprints show that dinosaur herds set out on lengthy journeys called migrations. They were probably moving north during the summer and south in the winter.

Safety in numbers

Paleontologists believe that Triceratops could have lived in family groups when young, but then became increasingly more solitary as they grew older. Vulnerable youngsters might have been protected by a parent or the herd until they could fend for themselves, at which point they would have broken away.

▼ Triceratops youngsters were easy prey for predators such as T. rex. Alone, they were very vulnerable.

Fossilized footprint

Huge herds

The long-necked sauropods traveled in large herds, sometimes numbering 100 or more. Some gathered with others of roughly the same age, while juveniles sometimes formed their own herds. Other herds were made up of individuals of all ages.

Hunting packs

Deinonychus may have hunted or scavenged in packs numbering about six or seven individuals, like wolves and hyenas do today. Hunting together meant that they could kill prey much larger than themselves.

T. rex on
the hunt

Lone hunters?

T. rex could have been either a loner or a pack hunter. We know that its close relative, Tarbosaurus, formed hunting packs. The younger members probably chased the prey, and the older ones delivered the fatal bite.

Vulnerable
prey

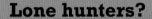

Hollow horns

The duck-billed dinosaur Parasaurolophus lived in herds. It had a pair of long, hollow, bony crests on top of its head, with tubes linking them to its nose. It may have used these to make trumpeting sounds and communicate with others in the herd.

Making more dinosaurs

Like most other male animals, male dinosaurs faced the challenge of getting close to females. This was because many females avoided close contact with others of their own kind, viewing them as being aggressive or as competitors for food and living space.

Males had to show females that they were fit and capable of fathering the strongest babies. They displayed showy crests, neck frills and horns, uttered loud calls, and fought rival males for breeding rights. It has even been suggested that sauropods had long necks because females were impressed by individuals with longer necks, and only mated with them. As a result, the necks just kept growing!

▲ Like battling deer stags, male Triceratops may have used their impressive horns to joust with other males to gain access to females.

Gender differences

The only reliable way of telling apart the sexes of dinosaurs is the presence of a special type of bone, known as the "medullary bone" in females. It has been found in at least three dinosaur species, including T. rex. Otherwise it is difficult to identify the sexes, as there are not enough fossils of a particular species to determine gender differences.

Head crests

The duck-billed dinosaur known as Lambeosaurus had a distinctive crest on its head. It is not known whether the males had a showier crest than females, but as the crest was hollow, it is thought that these dinosaurs could have made sounds that were intended to attract members of the opposite sex.

Feathery display

The birdlike theropod dinosaurs had feathers, and some had long tail feathers, like a peacock's tail. They might have used them for elaborate courtship displays, like those performed by some modern birds during the mating season.

Reproductive system

Many dinosaurs, including Triceratops, probably had a reproductive system that was anatomically similar to those of modern crocodiles. Males had testes to produce sperm and females had ovaries to produce eggs. Fertilization was internal, so mating was probably similar to that of modern crocodiles too.

▲ Scientists have noticed that T. rex females appear to be wider and larger than males, an adaptation perhaps for producing and laying eggs. But does that mean females competed for males, instead of the other way around? Nobody knows.

Eggs and nests

The latest findings suggest that all dinosaurs appear to have laid eggs.

Scientists also believe that the females of at least some dinosaur species cared for their eggs and young, just as birds and crocodiles do today. These dinosaurs created nests, and kept their eggs and young warm, dry, and away from danger.

Dinosaur egg types

Dinosaur eggs differ in size and shape depending on the species. The largest were about 160 times bigger than a chicken's egg. Prosauropod eggs were among the smallest, measuring just 3 inches across.

Titanosaur eggs
Some titanosaur eggs were round, measuring 4–5 inches across.

Oviraptor eggs
The eggs of this theropod were elongated and about 4–6 inches long.

Hadrosaur eggs
Some duck-billed dinosaur eggs were up to four times bigger than sauropod eggs.

Inside the egg

Scientists can sometimes see inside fossilized dinosaur eggs using scanners or by dissolving the eggshell away to reveal the embryo inside. Some of the best-preserved eggs are from Oviraptors. A mother was found in the brooding position, along with eggs containing embryos. They were probably all smothered by a violent sandstorm, which led to their fossilization.

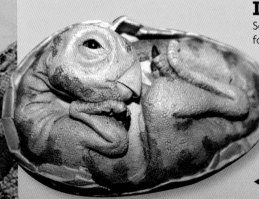

◀ Model Oviraptor egg and embryo

Nest types

Some eggs were laid in straight rows, and others in circles. Some were laid on flat ground, and others in high-sided pits. Nests were either covered in vegetation to keep the eggs warm and hidden, or covered by the mother, just like birds protect their eggs. This demonstrates how some dinosaurs were careful and precise.

▼ Fossils have been found of a mother Oviraptor nesting on her eggs. At first it was thought she was a predator raiding the nest, and not a nurturing mother-to-be.

▼A herd of Oviraptors in a nesting colony.

▼A model of a Maiasaura's nest, eggs, and hatchlings. The duck-billed dinosaur's name means "caring mother lizard."

Birth sites

Many dinosaurs, including theropods, sauropods, and hadrosaurs, nested in large colonies. Therizinosaur nests were laid out like modern seabird colonies, with each nest kept out of pecking distance of its neighbor. They used the same sites every year.

Growing up

It is possible that some dinosaur parents continued to care for their young after they hatched, much like crocodiles do today.

Some dinosaurs probably cared for their young, and others left them as soon as they were born. In fact, some babies were ready to leave the nest the moment they hatched, while others may have stayed together, needing protection from the rest of the herd. There were other babies that were nurtured by parents until they were big enough to survive on their own.

Baby Triceratops

Triceratops youngsters had little stubs for horns that curved back at first. As the animal grew, its horns straightened out, and once it matured the brow horns curved forward, reaching a length of about three feet.

Early breeders

It is thought that some dinosaurs, including T. rex, began having babies while they were still growing. In fact, many scientists believe that T. rex had a relatively short life span; some even died before they reached their maximum body size.

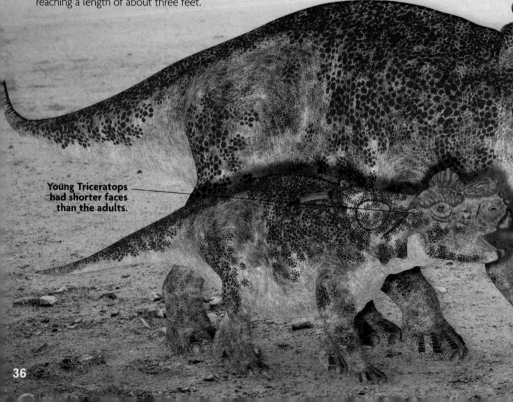

Young Triceratops had shorter faces than the adults.

At 14 years old, T. rexes had a growth spurt lasting two years.

Fighting skills

Young T. rexes probably had play-fights, practicing for real clashes in later life. Evidence for this comes from the fossil of a young dinosaur's snout. It has clear bite marks that had been caused by another young T. rex.

▲ Young tyrannosaurs having a play-fight

End of dinosaurs

About 65 million years ago, events took place on Earth that plunged all life into danger.

At the end of the Cretaceous period, Earth was affected by major changes to its environment. It may have taken only one of these changes to affect life on Earth, or perhaps a combination of several changes. Whichever the case, one thing is certain: it led to dinosaurs dying out, known as mass extinction.

Asteroids and volcanoes

It is generally accepted that dinosaurs became extinct after a large asteroid slammed into Earth. At the same time, huge and violent volcanic eruptions were happening all around, and the two combined, creating immense clouds of fine dust that blotted out the sun. Plants could not grow properly and food webs collapsed. All the dinosaurs eventually died out, along with much of the planet's wildlife.

▲ The killer asteroid was about 12 miles across and left a crater 110 miles in diameter near Chicxulub on Mexico's Yucatán Peninsula.

Lone survivors

A duck-billed dinosaur species appears to have survived long after all the other dinosaurs died out. Its thighbone was discovered in rocks that were laid down 700,000 years after the mass-extinction event. But this dinosaur eventually died out, too.

The inheritors

After the dinosaurs disappeared, several other groups of animals became the dominant species on Earth. Thought to be the natural descendants of dinosaurs (see below), birds grew to an immense size, with the giant "terror birds" taking over as one of the world's top predators. Snakes and crocodiles also grew big. In the 60-million-year-old swamps of South America, the 42-foot-long Titanoboa, a giant version of a modern constricting snake, grew longer than a bus. It competed for food with its 16-foot-long monster crocodile cousin called Anthrocosuchus.

▲ Terror birds were up to 10 feet tall and ran at 30 mph.

▲ Titanoboa lived like a modern anaconda.

▶ Dinosaurs had little chance of survival after large dust clouds blotted out the sun.

Dinosaur descendants

Dinosaurs are reptiles distantly related to modern lizards, snakes, and turtles, but the latest findings prove that some are more closely related to birds. For example, many scientists now believe that the meat-eating theropod dinosaurs were probably the ancestors of modern-day birds, which make birds "living dinosaurs."

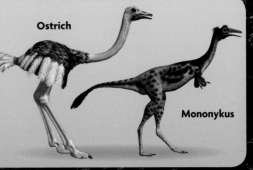

Ostrich

Mononykus

How your model fits together

Follow the instructions to make your Triceratops model. All the pieces are joined together by pegs, which fit into their corresponding peg holes.

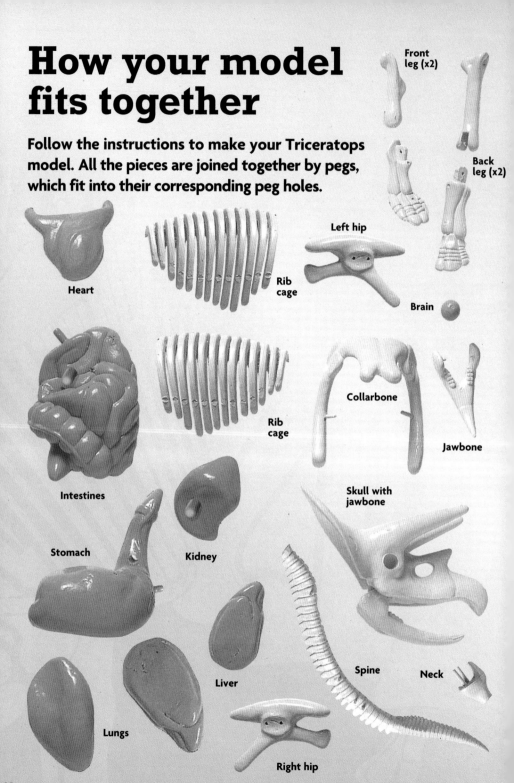

Front leg (x2)

Back leg (x2)

Heart

Rib cage

Left hip

Brain

Intestines

Rib cage

Collarbone

Jawbone

Stomach

Kidney

Skull with jawbone

Lungs

Liver

Spine

Neck

Right hip

1 Gather together all the body organs and lay them out in front of you as shown in the picture below. You should have intestines, a brain, a stomach, a liver, a kidney, right and left lungs, and a heart.

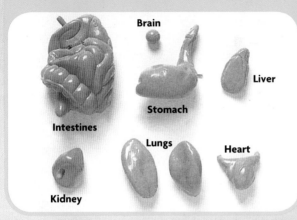

Brain

Liver

Stomach

Intestines

Lungs

Heart

Kidney

2 Take the intestines and the stomach and push the peg on the back of the intestines into the hole in the front of the stomach, so the stomach lies on top of the intestines.

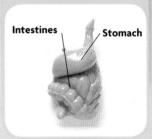

Intestines

Stomach

3 Fit the liver underneath the bottom end of the intestines. Then slot the peg at the back of the kidney into the hole in front of the stomach.

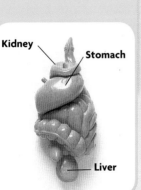

Kidney

Stomach

Liver

4 Fit the left lung onto the peg on the top side of the intestines. Then slot the right lung onto the peg on the side of the stomach. Now slot the heart onto the peg on the front of the kidney.

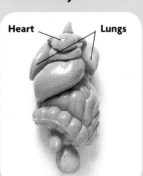

Heart

Lungs

5 The body organs should look like the picture below. The labels "head end" and "tail end" show you which way they should be attached to the spine.

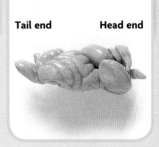

Tail end

Head end

6

Gather together the skeleton pieces. You should have two rib cage pieces, a neck, a spine, a brain, a skull, two hip bones, a collarbone, a jawbone, four front leg pieces, and four back leg pieces.

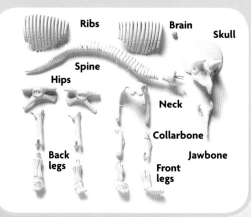

Ribs   Brain   Skull   Spine   Hips   Neck   Collarbone   Back legs   Jawbone   Front legs

7

Take the neck and the spine and join them together as shown. The spine has a small ball on one end, which fits into the socket on the end of the neck.

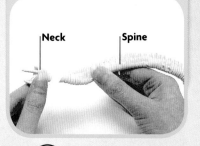

Neck   Spine

8

Hold the left side of the rib cage with the curved side facing away from you, and the small bones facing toward the tail of the dinosaur. Then push the pegs on the spine into the holes at the top of the rib piece.

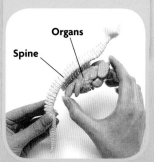

Spine   Left rib cage

9

Place the organs in the body cavity. Two pegs on the underside of the spine fit into the two holes on the back of the intestines. Make sure that the heart is at the head end of the spine, and the liver is at the tail end.

Organs   Spine

10

Take the right side of the rib cage and join it to the spine, as you did before with the left side (see step 8). The two rib cage pieces should both have the smaller ribs facing the tail end of your dinosaur.

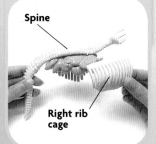

Spine   Right rib cage

11

Hold each hip bone with the longer end facing the tail end. Push the holes on the back of each hip into the pegs on the side of the spine.

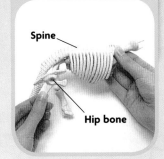

Spine

Hip bone

12

The back legs are longer than the front legs. Each leg has an upper (thigh) bone and a lower (shin) bone with a foot. Fit these two bones together to form your dinosaur's knee.

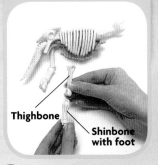

Thighbone

Shinbone with foot

13

The back legs join the skeleton at the hips, which are on each side of the spine. Push the peg at the top of each leg into the corresponding hole in the center of each hip bone.

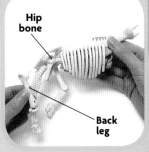

Hip bone

Back leg

14

Place the V-shaped collarbone around the front of the model. The pegs of the collarbone should fit neatly into the ribs.

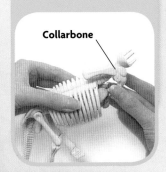

Collarbone

15

The front legs are shorter than the back legs. They are also made up of two bones. Join them in the same way as the back legs.

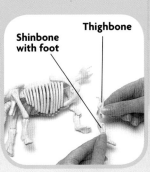

Shinbone with foot

Thighbone

16

Attach the front legs onto the collarbone by pushing the peg at the top of each leg into the hole on the side of the collarbone.

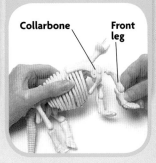

Collarbone

Front leg

17

The complete skull consists of an upper skull and a jawbone. These are already attached in your kit.

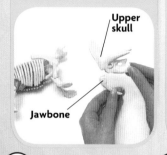

Upper skull

Jawbone

18

Place the brain inside the hollow of the neck bone. Push the two pegs on the front of the neck piece into the holes at the back of the skull.

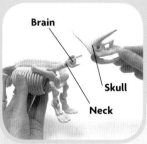

Brain

Skull

Neck

19

Place your complete dinosaur skeleton into the left side of the see-through skin.

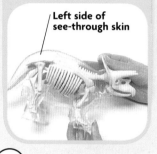

Left side of see-through skin

20

Join the four pieces of see-through skin to each side of the skeleton. Attach the piece of see-through skin that encloses the dinosaur's stomach. All the pegs on the outer edges of the skin pieces should snap shut tightly into the holes.

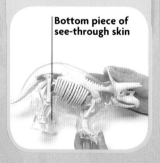

Bottom piece of see-through skin

21

Cover the whole body with the right side of the see-through skin. Again, the pegs on the outer edge of the skin should fit into the holes on the opposite piece. The model should stay shut when you lift it up.

Right side of see-through skin

22

Finally, place the last piece of the see-through skin over the skull. The horns and the jaw should poke through the holes at the front.

See-through head piece

(23) Your completed model Triceratops will look like this.

Make the card model

(1) Push the "forelimb" brace into the front slot of the organ piece, and the back brace into the tail slot so that the piece sits in the central grooves. Push the other two pieces into the braces, in the arrangement shown below.

(2) The T. rex's body should line up so that the skeleton is on one side, the skin on the other, and the muscles on the inside. Finally, slot in the two base pieces underneath.

Index

L
Lake Nyasa 3, 9
Lambeosaurus 33
large dinosaurs 3, 8, 14, 25
last dinosaurs 38
Leedsichthys 5
legs 11, 12, *see also* hind limbs
Liaoning, China 9
life span 36
lizards 12, 19, 25, 39
lungs 17

M
Maiasaura 35
male dinosaurs 32, 33
Mamenchisaurus 23
mammals 2, 4, 5
marine reptiles 4, 5
Masiakasaurus 19
mass-extinction events 38–39
mate attraction 24, 25, 26, 27, 29, 33
meat-eaters 2, 8, 11, 13, 15, 17, 18–19, 20, 24, 27, 28, 30, 39
medullary bone 32
Megalosaurus 8
Mesozoic era 2, 4–5, 9
Mexico 38
Microraptor 9, 24
migration 9, 30
Minmi 9
Mongolia 9
Mononykus 39
mosasaurs 5
movement coordination 14
mud 6, 7, 25
muscles 12–13

N
neck frills 11, 26, 32
necks, long 3, 4, 14, 15, 16, 17, 20, 23, 32
nervous system 14–15
nests 9, 18, 34–35
Nigersaurus 21
North America 2, 8, 9
Nyasasaurus 3, 9

O
olfactory region 14
omnivores 19
ornithischians 3
ornithopods 13
ostrich 39
ovaries 33
Oviraptor 19, 34, 35
Oxfordshire, England 8
oxygen 16, 17

P
Pachycephalosaurus 27
paleontology 6, 7, 24, 30, 31
Pangaea 2, 8
Parasaurolophus 31
parental care 34, 35, 36
Patagonia, Argentina 8
pigmentation 24, 25
plant-eaters 2, 8, 11, 13, 14, 15, 17, 18–19, 20, 21, 23, 26, 28
plants 18, 19, 23
plates 17, 28, 29
plesiosaurs 4
predation on dinosaurs 2, 5, 22, 30
prosauropods 34
Protoceratops 19, 26
pterosaurs 4

Q
Queensland, Australia 9
Quetzalcoatlus 4

R
Repenomamus 5
reproductive system 33
reptiles 4, 5, 12, 19, 39
running 13

S
sails 11, 17
sand 6, 34
saurischians 3
Sauropelta 28
sauropods 13, 14, 15, 17, 20, 21, 23, 31, 32, 34, 35

scales 25
scutes 26, 28
sea creatures 4–5
sediment 6
Sinosauropteryx 24
size 3, 4, 5, 7, 27, 28, 39
skeletons 5, 7, 10–11, 30, 32
skin 25
skulls 11, 26, 27
sleeping 11
small dinosaurs 9, 13
smell, sense of 14, 15
snakes 18, 25, 39
solitary hunting 30, 31
Solnhofen, Germany 8
sounds 31, 32, 33
South America 2, 8, 39
South Dakota 8
speed 12, 13, 39
spinal cord 14
spines 10, 11, 28, 29
Spinosaurus 9, 11, 17, 19
stegosaurs 6–7
Stegosaurus 17, 29
stomach 20
stones, gastric 20
"Sue" 8
swimming 4–5

T
T. rex *see* Tyrannosaurus rex
tail 3, 24, 28, 29
Tanzania 3, 9
Tarbosaurus 31
teeth 5, 11, 18, 21
temperature control 11, 17, 24, 29
tendons 29
terror birds 39
testes 33
Therizinosaurus 9, 19, 35
theropods 14, 17, 19, 20, 24, 27, 33, 34, 35, 39
thumbs 3
timeline 2
Titanoboa 39
titanosaurs 14, 16, 25, 34
tracks *see* footprints

Triassic period 2
Triceratops 2, 3, 7, 8, 9, 11, 12, 13, 14, 15, 16, 19, 20, 26, 30, 32, 33, 36–37
turtles 39
Tyrannosaurus rex 2–3, 8, 9, 10, 11, 13, 14, 15, 17, 18, 19, 22, 30, 31, 32, 33, 36–37

U
urine 22, 23

V
Velociraptor 13, 15, 19, 23
vertebrae 29
visual field 15
volcanoes 6, 38

W
warm-blooded dinosaurs 16, 17
waste products 22–23
water conservation 23
weight 12, 13

Y
young dinosaurs 5, 22, 30, 31, 36–37
Yucatán Peninsula, Mexico 38

Silver Dolphin Books

An imprint of Printers Row Publishing Group
10350 Barnes Canyon Road, Suite 100, San Diego, CA 92121
www.silverdolphinbooks.com

ISBN: 978-1-62686-566-2

Manufactured, printed, and assembled in Shenzhen, China
1 2 3 4 5 19 18 17 16 15

Author Michael Bright
Designer David Ball
Indexer Angie Hipkin
Editor Suhel Ahmed
Managing Editor Diane Pengelly
Creative Director Jonathan Gilbert
Publisher Zeta Jones

Picture credits (t=top, b=bottom, l=left, r=right, c=center, fc=front cover)

Alamy: 8b Nobumichi Tamura / Stocktrek Images, 14br inset The Natural History Museum, London, 20-21c
Leonello Calvetti / Stocktrek Images, 34l wonderlandstock, 34c, 34bl Sabena Jane Blackbird **Corbis:** 19b
Scientifica, I/Visuals Unlimited, 21br Alice Turner/Stocktrek Images **Getty Images:** 38-39c Mark Stevenson/
Stocktrek Images **Science Photo Library:** 6-7b JOSE ANTONIO PEÑAS, 12br LEONELLO CALVETTI,
22tr, 25tr, 35bc NATURAL HISTORY MUSEUM, LONDON, 24br, 35tr JULIUS T CSOTONYI, 30bl JAMES
STEINBERG, 32tr MARK HALLETT PALEOART, 34tr Dorling Kindersley/UIG **Shutterstock:** 2tr Designua,
2-3b Computer Earth, 3tl, 4tr, 4bl, 5br, 8tr, 9r, 14-15c, 23br, 24l, 29tr, 39tr, 39r Michael Rosskothen, 3tc, 4c,
5tr, 13tr, 13l, 14br, 21tr, 29tc, 31tl, 32-33b, 35br, 38bl Catmando, 3tr, 8tl, 15bc, 27b DM7, 4-5b Vilainecrevette,
6tr Redchanka, 7tr Darkkong, 7r mj007, 8l, 22-23c, 26t, 30-31cb, 35l Elenarts, 8bl, 8br, 13tl, 27t, 28tl, 28b, 33tr,
33l, 39br Linda Bucklin, 9tl, 26bl Valentyna Chukhlyebova, 9tr Herschel Hoffmeyer, 8-9c Gapchuk Lesia, 10l,
10-11bc, 15tl, 15tr dimair, 10-11b Radiokafka, 11rt CatbirdHill, 11rc Marques, 11rb Dinoton, 13tc 3Dalia, 16b
Frsenel, 17bl Aptyp_koK, 17br, 26br, 31tr Jaroslav Moravcik, 18c, 25c, 25b ExpressionImage, 18br Bob Orsillo,
19tl para, 19tc cyo bo, 19tr chungking, 20l Picsfive, 24tr Natursports, 28-29c Jean-Michel Girard, 28-29b Bruce
Rolff, 31br MarcelClemens, 36bl, 37tr Sofia Santos, 36-37b Cako, 37br Kostyantyn Ivanyshen, 38tr Mopic
All other illustrations by Nicholas Forder.
Additional graphics by D&A.